How to Grow and Use Lavender

A Comprehensive Guide in Growing and Using This Fragrant Herb

Margaret Green

ISBN-13: 978-1537249766

CONTENTS

AN INTRODUCTION TO LAVENDER

In this chapter we will be briefly discussing the history of lavender and talking about why someone would want to grow this herb in their garden.

A Brief History of Lavender

Lavender is an ancient herb. Its uses dating back over two thousand years from today and has been used throughout this time by a variety of cultures and civilizations. It is thought to have originated from the Mediterranean, Middle East and India. Lavender is an herb known for its iconic fragrance and is a flowering plant from the mint family.

The name Lavender is a descendant of the Latin word '*to wash*' or 'lavage' and found itself being used in ancient Rome for a multitude of tasks. Including as an herb for cooking as well as being added to water for bathing. Its use has been recorded on numerous other occasions, most notably, in the Bible. Mary even anointed Jesus with Lavender as a preparation for his burial.

This herb also had a part to play in the mummification process carried out by the Egyptians. Upon the discovery of ancient tombs there would often be traces of Lavender found in the decorative urns lining pyramids tombs floors.

To this day Lavender in continually grown and cultivated in its countries of origin, but has also spread across the globe.

So Why Grow and Harvest Lavender?

Lavender is one of the most recognizable fragrances bringing to mind imagery of childhood memory's filled endless summers that seemingly last forever. But if the smell alone isn't convincing enough, here are ten other reasons that I'm sure will show you why someone would want to grow and harvest lavender.

1. Overall Lavender is hardy plant.
   - It really doesn't require much attention as long as you choose the right variety to suit your conditions. Thriving in relatively harsh conditions is a big attraction to many growers.
2. Lavender's a natural Mosquito repellant properties.
   - While humans love its sent, certain insects including mosquitoes, moths and fleas are repulsed by its sweet smell in the garden. It's aroma can be added to clothes to keep you safe out and about.
3. To make Lavender Oil.
   - likely the most well-known of these ten points is that Lavender can be made into most versatile essential oil used for everything from dandruff, bee stings and even motion sickness.
4. Soothing stomachs using Lavender tea.
   - By using your dry harvested lavender and brewing an herbal tea you may find helpful in using lavender tea as a natural treatment for someone with an upset stomach.
5. Growing Lavender grows your hair.
   - It has been observed that the use of Lavender has been linked to hair growth. Studies have

shown that essential oils, when used during a daily head message, dramatically increase hair growth.

6. Making bath bombs
   - Throwing some Lavender into the mix when making your next batch of bath bombs will produce a beautiful smell as well as acting as a skin treatment.

7. Lavender homemade potpourri
   - By preserving you Lavender flowers as well as other things such as rose petals and orange peel you can make an amazingly fragrant potpourri to keep summers smells in your home all year round.

8. Lavender home décor
   - There are bundles of ways of turning your lavender plant into a piece of home décor that will really make your house into a home

9. Making Cocktails
   - Involving Lavender in your cocktails adds that summer feeling to any cocktail and is considered to be one of most stylish herbs in the world of cocktails.

10. Lilac Lemonade
    - A considered a true summer drink and a favorite by many this Lavender lemonade combo is an easy to make drink to be enjoyed by anyone.

The uses of Lavender are extensive, these ten reasons are really only scratching the surface as to why someone may choose to grow Lavender in their garden. So what do you think?

THE MOST COMMON SPECIES OF LAVENDER

In this section I will be mentioning the three of the most common species of Lavender. I will also be noting the characteristics of each species. I would encourage the reader to take the characteristics discussed into consideration when deciding on which variety of the Lavender plant will be most appropriate for you.

Lavandula Angustifolia

Lavandula Angustifolia or 'English Lavender' is the most common species of lavender. This species contains the Munstead and Hidcote varieties of Lavender. These two varieties are well recognized as some of the hardiest Lavender around. Some also call Lavandula Angustifolia 'true Lavender' for this reason as well as it being the most common Lavender.

This species can grow between half and one meter in height and like all Lavender its leaves are evergreen. Angustifolia is Latin for 'narrow leaf' and thus produces compact tidy plants which produce the highest quality oil for use in essential oils. The oils of Lavandula Angustifolia are often considered to be floral and sweeter than some other species.

These hardy plants will survive to below 5 degrees Fahrenheit and tend to start bloom throughout June and July and so are considered early bloomers. This species is also the parent of another of one of the other most common species of lavender 'Lavandula x Intermedia'.

Lavandula x Intermedia

Lavandula x Intermedia or 'Lavandin' is a hybrid plant, with its parents being the subspecies Lavandula Angustifolia (English Lavender) and Lavandula Latifolia (Spike Lavender) which is where the name Intermedia comes from. This species of Lavender produces a strong camphor smell which is known to be insect repellant and is even more robust than its notoriously hardy parent Lavandula Angustifolia. Popular varieties include Grosso and Abrialii.

This species can grow very large to over a meter in both height and width and its leaves are evergreen. This species produces enormous quantities of oil sometimes up to ten times more than Lavandula Angustifolia is seen to produce. However this oil is of a lesser quality when compared to Lavandula Angustifolia in terms of medicinal use.

These are the hardiest Lavender plants and will survive to well below 5 degrees Fahrenheit and below. They tend to start to bloom July through to August. This species is also a chef's choice when it comes to Lavender in the kitchen which could be something to keep in mind.

Lavandula Stoechas

Lavandula Stoechas is also known as 'French Lavender' or occasionally 'Spanish Lavender' is the more delicate of the three species we are discussing and is most well-known for its easily recognizable 'ears', which are actually bracts (modified leafs) that rest on the flowers head. They're color is a deep purple with light purple or pink 'ears'. This visually impressive lavender is becoming more popular as time goes on.

This species is a shorter one, general with heights between thirty and ninety centimeters. While producing a strong insect repellant smell this species doesn't not produce the quality or quantity of oil that some may desire.

As previously mentioned this species is less hardy than the other two and will only tolerate a minimum temperature of around twenty three degrees Fahrenheit for a few successive nights before Lavandula Stoechas begins to suffer. Deadheading its flowers, when done correctly, will allow the plant to bloom in May and nearly constantly flower through to September and sometimes October. I believe it to be the most beautiful of the three.

PLANTING AND BUYING LAVENDER

This section will cover all the things you need to know in regards to planting and growing your lavender plant. This section of the book should be used after you have considered which species of lavender you will be choosing to plant. The sections listed below are key in growing successful lavender plants.

Growing lavender from seed

It is very possible to grow lavender from seed however this is a far more time consuming and complex process when compared with purchasing a plant. I personally recommend buying a plant and skipping this section in its entirety. However if you are still intent on growing lavender from seed the process is as follows:

<u>What you will need</u>
- Lavender Seeds
- a sealable plastic bag
- seed starting soil
- a refrigerator
- a seedling tray (divided or undivided)
- potting mix
- large pots (minimum five centimeters diameter) or larger division free tray
- well-draining potting mix (soil and part peat, part perlite is preferable)
- granular slow-release fertilizer

You will also need a heating tray or an area with a temperature that will be consistently around seventy degrees Fahrenheit.

Germinating Seeds, you should begin this process six to twelve weeks before warm weather occurs. This is as lavender seeds can take up to a month to germinate and we want to ensure they are ready to develop into mature plants when the warm season comes around.

We begin this process by putting the seeds through a process known as 'cold stratifying', this process is designed to simulate a natural winter a seed would experience before it begins germination. Take your sealable plastic bag and place your desired amount of seeds in the bag. Then fill the bag with seed starting mix. Mix reasonably well with your hand to ensure an even distribution of seeds. Finally seal the bag and place the bag in your refrigerator for three weeks.

After these three weeks take your seedling tray and fill it with more seed starting mix. Remove your sealable bag from your refrigerator and pick out the seeds and placing them in the seedling tray. If your seedling tray is divided into pots, place one seed per pot. If your seedling tray is undivided place each seed around two centimeters apart. Then take your potting mix and sprinkle a small amount over the top of the seeds. No more than a third of a centimeter of soil, this layer of soil is to protect the seeds but at this stage the seeds will still require some sunlight in order to germinate. As just mentioned keep the seedling tray in a place inside with some sunlight. The temperature must consistently sit around seventy degrees Fahrenheit or on a heating mat at this temperature. Begin to lightly water the seeds every morning but only enough so that the soil will dry before each evening, over watering the seeds at this point will make the soil damp and be perfect conditions for fungus to grow and kill your seeds. Continue this process with patience as Lavender seeds can take up to a month to sprout.

After seeing the seeds sprout you must move your seedling container to an indoor location where it will receive plenty of direct sunlight. If there is no space you have fitting this position then placing them under a fluorescent lamps light for eight hours a day will be enough to simulate sun light and stimulate growth. This growth phase will end when each seedling shows its third set of 'true leaves'. These leaves are the first leaves that look like leaves of the full plant and will allow the plant to photosynthesize, when three sets of these leaves have been seen you may continue to the next step.

At this stage in the seedlings growth its root system will be beginning to get too large for a shallow seedling tray and so will have to be moved into a larger pot (minimum five centimeter diameter) or into a larger tray. Fill your container with well-draining potting mix, part soil, part peat and part perlite is preferable. Then take a small quantity of granular slow-release fertilizer and mix it in the soil in the container. When transplanting your lavender remember to only use one plant per pot or if using a larger tray, remember to leave five centimeter gaps between each plant. Then scoop out a small amount of dirt out of the larger pot or tray, the dirt removed should be similar to the height and depth of the soil the seedling is currently in. Carefully remove each lavender plant from its seedling tray and transplant it into its new container each time packing the soil to keep each plant firmly situated. Allow the lavender to continue growing in this state until the plant has reached a height of seven and a half centimeters, at this stage the plants should only have a single stem. This could take up to three months.

The last thing to do is to acclimatize your lavender plants

to being outside, each day take your plants outside and leave them in partial sunlight for a number of hours. Doing this will allow the lavender plants to get used to their new living conditions. You will want repeat this process for a week or so and then, finally, you will be at a stage when your plants are ready to grow outdoors in their final destination.

Buying Lavender Plants

This section will cover information detailing what to look for when you are purchasing your lavender plants to ensure that they are high quality plants. Lower quality plants will occur more in the delicate species of lavender such as Lavandula Stoechas, so if you are choosing a plant like this I would encourage you to be particularly cautious when purchasing your plants.

Condition: Checking the leaves of your lavender plant for unusually pale green leaves, dry foliage, yellowing or wilting of leaves are all signs of a plant to steer clear of. These indicate a low quality plant. Another thing to check for are holes or ragged edges of the leafs as these will tell you pests have gotten to the plant. What you want to be looking for is even growth of all areas of the pot with mature green leaves.

Mosses: The next thing I would check for would be the presence of mosses and liverworts on the soil of the container. The presence of moss and liverworts would show that your plant is very old stock and so may not be a prime example a high quality plant. Older stock may already be in flower and are more likely to suffer from being root bound.

Check the roots: Another thing to check for is mentioned briefly above. Try and knock the plant gently to remove it from the pot. The first sign of a root bound plant will be that it is hard to remove from its pot. Once removed from its pot a high quality lavender plant will have its roots tightly filling the pot, but not creating circles or with roots that are very densely packed. This means avoid plants where the roots are packed to the point where little soil is visible at the base and edges of the plants roots.

Flower buds: While fully flowering lavender may be the most tempting to purchase I would recommend selecting a flowerless plant or a plant with very tight buds. By choosing a plant as described you are ensuring that when the plant reaches its final destination, its growth is focused more on root and leaf growth than flower growth. This is beneficial as it will allow the plant to be better situated in its final location in terms of its root system. It will also allow the lavender to be flowering in the final location for a longer period of time.

When to Plant Your Lavender

It is recommended to plant your lavender during the months of April and May or as the soil begins to warm for lavenders more hardy varieties. This is due to its tough nature and thus its ability to thrive in fairly poor conditions, however for more delicate varieties only plant your lavender once you're sure cold weather has passed.

Where to Plant Your Lavender

As mentioned in the 'history of lavender' section, lavender is originally a Mediterranean plant and so it thrives in sunlight. You must choose a place in your garden where the lavender will be in the sunlight for a minimum of eight hours a day. You should also plant your lavender somewhere that is reasonably well protected from the wind. If possible plant your lavender near a store or a wall, this will provide extra heat and shelter for the lavender plant.

What Soil Is Best For Your Lavender

Your choice of soil is an important factor in the life of your lavender plant. Dampness is arguably lavenders greatest enemy and so you should choose a location in your garden or use a soil that lightly packed and well-aerated. This will ensure that the soil has enough drainage and will be the optimum lavender growing conditions. Damp conditions will increase of fungus growing and destroying the root system of your plant. To increase the amount of drainage you can add grit to more heavy soil to aerate it. You can also plant your lavender on a raised bed or on top of a slope to increase drainage. Wet soil is what will most commonly kill a lavender plant

Lavender also prefers neutral and slightly alkaline, or chalky, soils. You can test this by using a commercial test probe and looking for a value around six and a half and no more than seven. If your result is above seven add some pine sawdust, if your result is much below six and a half add some agricultural lime to your soil. About a handful per square meter will be sufficient quantities of either material to alter the soils pH level. Contrasting the above statements Lavandula Stoechas has been known to thrive in acidic conditions in the wild. However I should also note I will still recommend you to used slightly alkaline soil in your garden for the best possible results.

I would not recommend adding any plant food to your lavender plants as I will once again say lavender thrives in harsher conditions.

Spacing Your Lavender Plants

For spacing half a meter for most average sized lavenders, this would be prefect spacing for Lavandula Angustifolia and would be slightly too large for Lavandula Stoechas. For larger species and varieties such as Lavandula x Intermedia spacing of an over half a meter would be appropriate.

Planting lavender in groups of three is known to be an effective method of grouping for creating lavender hedging. Lavandula Angustifolia and Lavandula x Intermedia are the perfect plants to use as hedging in this way and create a stunning effect.

Planting In Pots

Planting in pots is most appropriate for more delicate species of lavender such as Lavandula Stoechas or other types of dwarf lavender. Thirty to forty centimeter diameter pots would be most appropriate for the lavender plants. Water your lavender in its current nursery pot at least eight hours before planting you lavender, this will ensure the plant is hydrated but not damp before going into its pot. Fill your pot with the soil type as discussed in the previous section and add a few plugs of slow release fertilizer, this should be all the plant food your lavender plant will need. Take your trowel and dig a hole in the center of your pot deep and wide enough to contain your plants roots.

Prune your lavender before planting to encourage growth and stem health as well as providing good air circulation to the stems. Details on pruning your lavender can be found in another section of this book.

Next you will need to prepare the roots. After removing the plant from its nursery pot careful shake the plant to remove any soil from its previous home. Planting the lavender without this soil or with bare roots will ensure it situates itself into its new environment as fast as possible.

Place the lavender in the hole you previously dug laying your soil mix over the plants roots, fill the hole and lightly pack the soil over the roots. After this you have now successfully planted your lavender.

Planting Elsewhere

This process is very similar to planting in pots the only difference being taking into account the distance between your plants. First water your lavender a minimum of eight hours before planting before planting your lavender, this allows the plants roots to not be damp but also hydrated before going into its bed. Ensure the soil type where you are going to plant your lavender is as discussed in the previous section and mix a few slow release fertilizer granules into the soil, these few granules will be all your plant needs for the rest of the season. Dig a hole with your trowel at the center of where you want your plant to grow, as deep and wide enough to contain your plants roots. If planting multiple lavender plants please remember to leave adequate spacing as discussed in the 'spacing your lavender plants' section of this book.

Next you should prune your lavender. Pruning your lavender before planting will allow better stem health and growth while also giving the plant great air circulation around its stems. The pruning process for lavender is describe in far greater detail later in this book.

Preparing the roots is the next step. Remove your lavender from its pot and softly shake the plant until the majority of the soil around its roots has fallen off. With roots bare it is seen that the lavender plant will quickly adapt to being in its new surroundings and aid growth.

Take your plant and place it in the aforementioned hole, fill and lightly pack the hole and roots down with your soil mix. Finally your lavender plant is in the ground and you have planted your lavender.

GROWING AND MAINTAING YOUR LAVENDER

So you have planted your lavender, we will now discuss all of the things you need to do to grow and maintain your plant. As you will see, one of the advantages of lavender is as with the right care the plant is very low maintenance and so can be grown with minimal effort.

Fertilizing your Soil

You will only really need to fertilize your plant a few times a year. First I will describe the spring fertilization, to do this take a mix of compost and bone meal and use this as a light top layer around the base of the plant. You should also feed your lavender with a seaweed extract or liquid fish emulsion a few times over the course of the summer for the best possible results. This process will lead your plant to being more winter hardy which is important if you are growing your lavender in beds.

Watering Your Lavender Plant

During the lavenders first year in a bed or if a lavender plant is potted please follow these rules for watering your lavender. Very lightly water your plants every morning so that the soil will dry the same day, if the soil remains wet for longer than this do not water the plant anymore and wait for the soil to dry. For potted plants follow these instructions for all of summer. For newly bedded plants follow these instructions for around three weeks.

The attitude taken to watering an established lavender

plant should be 'less is more.' Lavender is very drought resistant and shall not require watering after a few weeks of the plant being its bed. However during weeks of exceptionally dry weather you should water the lavender plant. The plant should be watered in the morning very lightly everyday so that the soil will dry by the evening.

During the winter do not water your lavender plants. Wait until the plants wilt, or their pot is noticeably lighter. Water extremely lightly during this period and only water the soil, not over the leaves of the plant. Lavender in beds are very unlikely to need watering during the winter months however you may choose to add a mulch of bark or gravel around the base of your plants to keep them warm during the winter months. If you choose to use bark mulch or add gravel remember to leave around fifteen centimeters around the base of the plant empty to ensure good airflow is still ensured.

A sign of over watering would be the soil staying wet for day's consecutive days after watering the plant. With heat and humidity fungus could have a chance of growing and attacking and killing your plants, this would be seen by the leaves of your plant turning brown. In fact during spring overwatering your lavender plants is the main cause of a plant failing.

Preventing Weeds

A simple and effective method for deterring weeds from taking seed near your lavender plant is adding mulch to your soil. By using a light colored mulch such as coarse sand or gravel you will keep weeds well away from your lavender.

Pests and Your Lavender Plant

Due to how hardy lavender plants are they are generally trouble free if grown in the correct conditions. Lavender plants can tolerate and survive most pests. However are not completely invulnerable. A list of the pests is as follows:

Aphids: These well-known pest do not pose a direct threat to your lavender but can carry the alfalfa mosaic virus which is recognizable by yellow patches on the plants leaves and shoots. This disease will not kill your lavender plant but will however reduce further growth and blooming of the plant. It is recommended to uproot and burn any plant carrying this virus as it can spread to other plants where it may be more dangerous. To prevent this disease you must control aphid populations. This is achieved by cleaning gardening tools, introducing a natural predator, pruning aphid infested stems and using pesticides. When using a pesticide it is preferred to use an organic pesticide as some chemical pesticides have an effect on the oil production of your lavender plant.

Spittle Bugs: These bugs are common during the spring time and will be recognized by leaving a foamy substance, with an appearance like 'spittle', on the lavender plant. These pets are unlikely to cause your plant much harm however are still best removed. In more extreme cases the stem the spittle bugs will sometimes die. During spring, when these pests are most present, spray your plant with a strong spray of water, this is easily remove all of the spittle bugs and their spittle.

Whiteflies: These pests feed on its host plants sap and can yellow the leaves of you lavender plant, the honeydew that is left following whiteflies can in some cases cause sooty mold. The most effective treatment for a whitefly infestation would be the introduction of one of its natural predators. One such predator is Delphastus pusillus which is a type of lady bird that will feed on whiteflies and shall solve your problem should this issue arise. Strong sprays of water will help somewhat if an infestation should occur, but may not solve the issue.

Pruning Your Lavender Plant

During lavenders first year it will grow slowly due to the fact a lot of the plants energy will be going towards developing its root systems and negative growth. This process can be encouraged by cutting off any steam once its buds have started to open. You should leave behind a third of new growth each time you cut the flowering stems. By doing this in the first year you will obtain a tidy round plant for later years. This is uniform for the first year however after this point pruning depends on the species of lavender that you are growing.

Hardy lavender such as Lavandula Angustifolia and Lavandula x Intermedia will only produce one full flush of flowers. After flowering prune the lavender plant so that its stems are around twenty centimeters long. This is important to the plants growth and is particularly important with the Lavandula x Intermedia variety. After pruning you should see small shoots visible amongst the trimmed stems, this indicates a successful plant confirmation of your plant flowing the following year. If pruned correctly over winter your lavender should turn to hummocks. Lavender varieties of a hard nature can be expected to las over twenty years if pruned correctly.

For more tender lavenders such as Lavandula Stoechas you will want to prune the flowers back to twenty centimeters after the first flowers have shown. After that point you plant will produce flowers all through summer if deadheaded during the flowering period and plants will tend to flower into early September. A light trim after the last flowers begin to wilt will prepare this type of lavender for winter. After this trim the plant you will be able to see new shoots if the plant will be flowering next year. These types of lavender can be expected to last between five and ten years with proper pruning.

PROPAGATING YOUR LAVENDER PLANTS

In this section of the book we will be discussing different ways to propagate your lavender plants. We will cover softwood and hardwood cuttings as well as collecting lavender seeds. I should note that lavender seeds will not be exact clones on the parent plant and so cuttings may be more appropriate for some growers.

Collecting Lavender Seeds

Collecting lavender seeds is a very simple process. The lavender seeds are found within the lavender head. Do not deadhead one of your flowers and let the head dry out on the plant. You will know the plant is dry enough when you can shake the flower head and seeds will fall out.

To collect your seeds you have two options. You can take a container and shake the flower heads over it. Or you can cut the off the flower head place them into a container, then shake the container till all the seeds have fallen out of the heads. You will then need to remove the flower heads.

After you have collected your seeds there are is going to be plant matter that has fallen into your container as well as the seeds, pick these out. You now have seeds ready to sow, please look at the 'growing lavender from seed' section of this book if you would like to read a detailed guide of what it takes to grow lavender from seed.

Softwood Cuttings

Taking softwood cutting occurs in spring or sometimes early summer and are known to be less reliable than hardwood cuttings. If the cutting is potted by midsummer the plant will grow enough and develop enough roots to survive the winter, and will flower the following year.

We will be making a cutting just below the leaf joint (or node) on a stem with no flowers. This part of the plant has a large concentration of root production hormones. Take your knife and cut a section of the stem just below the leaf node and then trim the other end so the cutting in around five to ten centimeters long. Remove any lower leaves from the lower five centimeters of the stem and then also scrape the skin off of this portion of the cutting.

Then take a small pot and fill it with a mix of half vermiculite and half peat moss or perlite. You can also dip the nodal end into a rooting hormone to aid its rooting, however this is not necessarily needed due to lavenders hardy nature.

Take your cutting and place it so five centimeters of the cutting are below the soil. Then place your container inside a plastic bag. Softwood cuttings can take up to a month to root. To check to if your cutting has rooted you can gently tug the stem of the cutting and you will feel resistance if a root structure exists.

Once a root system has developed remove the plastic bag. During the next two or three weeks it is advised to your new plant with one quarter strength liquid fertilizer After two of three weeks you may need to transplant the cutting to prevent the plant from becoming root bound. At this stage your cuttings are now ready to be planted in your garden or moved into a larger container to grow over the remaining summer.

Hardwood Cuttings

Using hardwood cuttings as a method of propagating lavender is in my opinion the most effective method. This process will can occur just after leaf fall and also immediately before bud-burst (which is at the beginning for spring when new shoots begin to show). This considered to be an easier process than softwood cuttings, despite this method being slower it is known to be the most consistent method of propagation for lavender.

Select a healthy shoot that has shown good growth during the year and that has become rigid and inflexible, they should be as thick as a pencil. Remove the soft section of growth from the plants length. Find the leaf joint or node on the stem and cut the stem of just below this point. Cut the stem into sections that are fifteen to thirty centimeters long. Also make one end of each section sloped so you can tell which end is going to be placed into the ground.

Take a smaller pot and fill it with gritty compost. Dip the base end of your cutting into rooting powder and then place it in your pot. For hardwood cuttings place the cutting twelve to fifteen centimeters deep into the pot. This will cause roots to grow along the stem. Some buds should remain above the ground to allow the plant to still be able to grow in spring.

These cuttings will take a full year until they are able to be planted in a bed. During the summer water as appropriate, but remember considerations regarding watering as discussed in the 'watering your lavender plant' section of this book.

HARVESTING YOUR LAVENDER

This section will be a guide to harvesting your lavender for drying and for display. Dried lavender is used for a number of purposes, most notably you will you dried lavender in the production of lavender oil. Fresh lavender can be harvested and make great addition to a wide range of indoor flower arrangements.

Harvesting Lavender for Decoration

When harvesting your lavender for a fresh flower display in your home there are a number of factors you need to take into account. These are considered in order to optimize the harvest process as well as the longevity of your cut lavender. Also take into account that pruning and harvesting are very similar processes.

The first factor in the decision to harvest your lavender should be at what stage of growth is your lavender plant? Most flowers are harvested just as they begin to show color, however for lavender it is recommended to harvest just as the buds begin to open.

Once your buds are beginning to open you are ready to cut your lavender. This process is best carried out during the morning, this is as the plants stem will be turgid (full of water) and after the dew has dried. To cut your lavender for display take a cutting down above the leaf joint or node. As previously mentioned harvesting your lavender in this way will encourage health growth. When cutting lavender it is advised to use a sickle, taking bundles of the plant in your hand and cutting in this way will be a very quick way to harvest your lavender.

After you have a bunch of lavender, place it down and continue harvesting all of your lavender.

Once you have harvested all of your lavender you will need to prepare cut plants before they go into their vase. This will both help the visually aid the flowers as well as help in prolonging their life. Firstly strip any leaves from the stem that are going to be below the water level inside of your vase, this will prevent the plant matter from rotting in the vase. You may want to further cut down your stem depending on the height of your vase, this will also improve their ability to absorb nutrients and water from the vase. When cutting your flowers this time make sure to make an angled cut at the base of the stem, ensure that the cut is clean as any remaining plant matter could rot in the vase.

After preparing your lavender in this way place them in a bucket of water overnight or for a minimum of three hours. These steps will make sure that your lavender is ready to be placed in your chosen flower arrangement.

Harvesting and Drying Lavender

Harvesting and drying your lavender is very popular as it allows growers to utilize their lavender to its full potential. You should harvest your lavender just as they bloom which will most likely be in spring, this will mean that you will most likely get a second full harvest of lavender later in the season. By gathering lavender in bunches in your hand and cutting the lavender plant a few inches above the woody growth. This job is best carried out with a sickle. After you cut a bunch of lavender make sure you have rubber bands handy to wrap around the bunch, this is done simply to keep the bunches together and so helps in preparation for the drying process

Pruning and harvesting your lavender for drying are identical processes. So for a more detailed guide to harvesting your lavender see 'pruning your lavender plant' and 'harvesting lavender for decoration'. After you have your lavender bunches there are a few methods of drying your lavender.

The first method is taking your bundles of lavender and tying them upside-down, they can be tied with string or hung from a nail. You can do this method for each smaller bundle or group smaller bundles if this is more convenient, however grouping the bundles could take more time. This method can also be done indoors or outdoors if you do not have the space. Drying inside is recommended to be done in a dry, dark and cool place. This is seen as the preferred method as it allows the lavender to retain more of its natural color as well as hold more of its oils. Drying outside may be faster but, as just mentioned, you will lose some color and some of the lavenders oil to the sun's rays.

Another method of drying if you do not have a suitably dark place is placing bundles in brown paper bags. By cutting slits in the bag sides you will add air circulation and create a dry cool environment with good airflow. Drying lavender in this way means you can place your drying lavender all over your house, if you love the smell of lavender this would be a good method for you.

After two to four weeks of leaving your lavender it should have fully dried. Once dry you can de-stem your lavender by shaking or gently rubbing the stems and flowers to a container. You can now store this lavender in a closed jar in a dark place or use the dried lavender for whatever you want.

USING YOUR LAVENDER

So now you wonder what I can do with my lavender. this section of the book will detail just a few ideas of things you could do with your lavender including a guide to making lavender oil.

Benefits of Using Lavender Oil

Lavender oil is the most popular essential oil in the world and science has only recently begun studying and evaluating its health benefits. Below I have listed a number of the health benefits of using lavender oil.

One use of lavender oil that which I have found most useful is its property's in relieving headaches. A study published in the 'European Journal of Neurology' tested using lavender oil in a group of people suffering with migraines. Subjects felt a significant reduction in pain after inhaling lavender oil as treatment. In my opinion the most effective method for alleviating headaches is taking four drops of lavender oil in the palm of your hands and rubbing the oil into your temples, forehead and back of your neck. This combined with Inhalation has always greatly eased my pain and could recommend it to anyone. In order to inhale your lavender take a bowl of hot water and add four to six drops of lavender oil. Then place your head over the bowl and a towel over your head and inhale for as long as needed.

Another use of this wonderful oil is lavender oils benefit on the skin. By adding ten drops of lavender oil to an ounce of aloe or coconut oil you have produced a product capable of aiding the healing of minor cuts and grazes, as well as dramatically aiding in the healing process of even the worst sunburn.

Throughout history lavender has been used to treat issues such as depression and anxiety and has more recently been backed up by a clear medical study carried out by the 'International Journal of Psychiatry in Clinical Practice'. In this study it was found that using eighty milligram doses of lavender essential oil had a significant effect on subject's anxiety and depression. It should also be noted that there are no negative side effects from using lavender oil in this way, as opposed to modern pharmaceutical drugs used in the treatment for these conditions.

Another use of lavender oil is in settling stomach discomfort. People who are experiencing nausea often find the smell of lavender soothing to them. So if you experience motion sickness spraying lavender oil on your skin and clothes can greatly reduce your nausea.

One other use of lavender oil is for its antioxidant properties. A substance is said to be an antioxidant if it prevents oxidants from causing damage to your body. Oxidants are produced to protect yourself against viruses and disease but when created in excess can cause serious damage to your body. A Romanian study showed after inhaling lavender oil for sixty minutes a day people were far more protected from cell damage that could lead to cancer.

Another traditional use of lavender is in its properties in reducing insomnia. You can do this by using an 'aromatherapy diffuser' or if you don't fancy that you can also simply sprinkle a few drops of lavender oil on a piece of tissue and place it under your pillow. Researchers have found during studies that lavender has properties that allow it to help induce and slow-wave or deep sleep. This deep sleep is defined by characteristics of decreased heartbeat and greater amounts of muscle relaxation. This type of sleep is the most important and will leave you feeling more energetic when you arise in the morning.

Making Lavender Oil

This guide will begin at a stage after you have harvest dried and de-stemmed your lavender, to find details of this process please read the 'harvesting your lavender' section of this book. For this guide you will need a jar large enough to hold your lavender and oil, a cheese cloth and a dark bottle.

The first step is to take your lavender and gently crumble it in your hands, this step will simply increase the surface area of the lavenders contact when sitting in the oil and so will optimize the diffusion process.

Now choose your oil, you should choose an oil which is non-scented and lightly colored, common oils in the production of lavender oil are almond oil, olive oil and safflower oil. Using a non-scented oil will ensure your final product is as fragrant as possible.

Next take your jar and place your dried lavender inside it. Add your chosen oil. Add only enough oil to fully cover your lavender and ensure there is around two inches of space empty at the top of your jar, this is as the oil will expand as the plant matter takes on the oil. Then close the jar.

Leave this jar to soak in a sunny place for three to six weeks, this will leave the enough time for the oil to take on the desired properties of the lavender. If you don't have time for this you can choose to double boil your oil. Remove the lid of your container and start double boiling your oil. Your should do this for two to five hours and ensure the mixture is at a steady temperature of one hundred to one hundred and twenty degrees Fahrenheit.

After soaking your lavender strain your oil from the lavender using your cheesecloth into another container. Then remove the plant matter from your cloth. At this stage your oil can either be stored or you can repeat the process of soaking or double boiling again in order to create a stronger oil.

Optionally you can add a few drops of vitamin E oil. Adding the vitamin E oil has the advantage of increasing the shelf life of your lavender oil. Add a few drops of vitamin E oil and stir well to ensure the oils are properly mixed.

Finally store your oil in a dark jar or bottle. This will help your oil have the maximum shelf life it can. This bottle should be kept in a dark cool location to aid the oil keeping its aroma from breaking down. If kept in these conditions your lavender oil can last for months.

Making Lavender Potpourri

This is a quick and easy potpourri that will leave your home with a smell of lavender wafting through the air. For this potpourri you will need two or three cups of dried lavender, half a teaspoon of orris rooting powder, some lavender oil and a glass jar.

Firstly take your lavender, orris powder then add around twenty drops of lavender oil and place them into a jar. Shake the jar so all the oil is absorbed and the powder is mixed in. Orris powder will help set the smell making your potpourri fragrance around for longer. Leave your soon to be potpourri in the jar with the lid on for a week, shaking daily. It's also advised to keep the jar out of sunlight as much as possible. This is as sunlight can hurt the aroma of your potpourri.

After this your potpourri is complete and you can place it into a decorative container, or place in sachets. Personally I prefer to leave my potpourri in an open dish in my room of choice. Another good idea is to add some dried rose petals to add to the appearance of your potpourri.

Making Lavender Wands

Lavender wands are more complex to make when starting out however they are indisputably more visually appealing and are truly a pleasure to see around the house. For each wand you will need an odd number (but at least thirteen) fresh lavender stems, each being twelve inches tall. These will be harvested just after the flowers bloom in and in the morning, this is to ensure the stems are supple enough to survive the wand making process. You will also need around three yards of a quarter inch ribbon.

First you will need to remove all leaves along the stem, then take your ribbon and tie them around the bottom of the bundle of flower heads. Hold the bundle upside down and carefully bend the stem over the tops of the flower heads and back round to where the ribbon is tied. If your stems are stiff you can take the flat side of a spoon and gently crush them to make the stems more supple. The aim of this is to produce an evenly spaced cage around the flower heads, you must also ensure that the flower steams do not overlap as this will cause aggravation at a later stage.

The next step is to take your ribbon and begin weaving it in and out of your cage, pulling the ribbon after each weave to ensure the ribbon is tight. Continue weaving the ribbon into the stems until you have covered all of the flowers. Once you have finished wrapping cage in ribbon tie off the ribbon or use a rubber band and cut the stems to length if they are too long.

Now your lavender wand is ready to be hung up around the house and will give off its gentle aroma for years to come. If your want has stopped producing a smell, give the wand a gentle squeeze and it will begin giving of its fragrant smell once again.

Tips for Cooking With Lavender

Lavender can be used to great effect within cooking however there are somethings to keep in mind. When cooking with lavender remember to cook with culinary grade lavender or if using your own lavender remember to consider if you have used any herbicides pesticides or any other substance on your lavender that may make its harvest not fit for consumption, this includes substances used before you bought the plant as well as residual substances in your soil that your plant may have ingested. If unsure I would err on the side of caution and just purchase culinary lavender.

Another tip I can give you is to ensure to fully grind your lavender when adding it into your dishes. This is as lavender is, more often than not, used in baking and I cannot imagine eating a cake with leafy bits being pleasant. Alternatively you could strain your mixture if you choose to use larger pieces of lavender.

If you don't have much experience with cooking using lavender or are trying a new recipe I would definitely recommend using lavender sparingly. This is even small amounts of lavender have a tremendous amount of flavor and can easily overpower any other flavors you may be trying to incorporate into your meal. It is very easy to turn a lovely dessert or meal into an experience more like eating potpourri which is not an enjoyable experience.

Another tip that is in relation to lavenders strong flavor is to pair its taste with another assertive flavor, by this I mean a flavor such as lemon. This can greatly compliment the lavenders taste and in terms of savory dishes goes wonderfully with lamb and chicken. If you're looking to experiment with lavender some other flavors I can recommend are: blueberries, strawberries, lemon, honey, sage, orange, thyme, black pepper, oregano and rosemary.

My personal favorite recipe is lavender shortbread. Adding one or two teaspoons of dried and ground lavender to my usual shortbread recipe I've found it effective in providing me with a hint of floral flavor as well as a giving the short bread a gentle lavender smell.

Another recipe I've grown fond of is lavender lemonade, for this you will need one cup of raw honey, five cups of water, one quarter cup of dried lavender or one drop of lavender oil, six lemons peeled and juiced.

Take two and a half cups of water and bring it to a boil, then remove it from the heat and add your dried lavender or drop of oil as well as your honey. Leave the mixture for twenty minutes, then strain the mixture into a larger container and your lemon juice and your remaining water. Finally mix and your lavender lemonade is complete, now add ice refrigerate and drink.

Printed in Great Britain
by Amazon